# PEOPLE of the CANYON

## By Suzanne Weyn

**Modern Curriculum Press**
*Parsippany, New Jersey*

**Credits**

**Photos:** All photos © Pearson Learning unless otherwise noted.

Front cover: Stephen Trimble. Title page: Justine Locke/National Geographic Image Collection. 5: David Muench/Corbis. 7: Mark Newman/Bruce Coleman Inc. 9: Pat O'Hara/Corbis. 11: Jack W. Dykinga/Bruce Coleman Inc. 13: Stephen Trimble. 14: SuperStock, Inc. 15, 16: Tom Bean. 18: Florence Baker Collection, Cline Library/Northern Arizona University. 19: John K. Hillers/Corbis. 20: Hulton Getty/Liaison International. 21, 23: Bill Belknap Collection, Cline Library/Northern Arizona University. 24: U.S. Geological Survey. 26–27: NOAA Photo Library, U.S. Department of Commerce. 29: Corbis. 30: Henry Peabody/Corbis. 31: Tom Bean. 32, 33: AP/Wide World Photos. 34, 35: Justine Locke/National Geographic Image Collection. 36, 37: Bill Belknap Collection, Cline Library/Northern Arizona University. 38: Tom Bean. 40: Stephen Trimble. 42: Tom Bean. 43: Layne Kennedy/Corbis. 44, 47: Tom Bean.

Cover and book design by John Maddalone

**Modern Curriculum Press**
An imprint of Pearson Learning
299 Jefferson Road, P.O. Box 480
Parsippany, NJ 07054–0480

*www.pearsonlearning.com*

1-800-321-3106

ISBN 0-7652-2154-3

2 3 4 5 6 7 8 9 10 11  MA  07 06 05 04 03 02 01

# CONTENTS

To Diana Gonzalez,
who is always exploring
something new

# chapter 1

# Life in a Secret Canyon

Imagine spending the afternoon swimming in a pool of sparkling blue-green water at the bottom of a giant waterfall. On your way home you can walk in the middle of the road if you want. It's safe because there are no cars.

As you walk down the road, you see the mail carrier leading a mule team into town. The mules carry the mail for you and your neighbors. You wave to many friends as you go.

**Mooney Falls in Havasu Canyon**

This would be your life if you were a child in the Havasupai (hav uh SOO pye) tribe of Native Americans. They are the smallest Native American nation in America. As of 1997 there were 639 official members.

To visit the Havasupai, you would have to go to the Grand Canyon in northern Arizona. The Colorado River rushes through the bottom of the canyon. It has cut the surrounding rock to form steep canyon walls. The rock is striped red and orange. Areas of dry, flat land called plateaus surround the tops of the canyon walls.

The Havasupai make their home in a remote side canyon called Havasu Canyon and on the plateaus above it. Living so far from other people has helped the Havasupai keep their traditional ways of life for hundreds of years.

Travel to Havasu Canyon has always been difficult. From the plateaus the canyon home of the Havasupai is eight miles down a steep trail that winds along the rugged canyon walls. At one time the Havasupai used a dozen trails leading from the plateaus to the canyon floor. Today there are only two trails open to the public that lead to Supai (SOO pye), the Havasupai town.

Other trails cross burial grounds and other areas that the Havasupai believe are sacred or spiritual. To preserve these areas, the Havasupai don't want anyone from the outside world walking through them.

The Havasupai also won't allow any of the trails in the canyon to be made into roads large enough for cars. Roads and cars would spoil the land's quiet beauty. So the only ways down the trails are still by foot, horse, or mule.

**Pack mules carry supplies down the canyon trail.**

Even though the canyon is difficult to get to, it has become one of the most popular and spectacular vacation spots in the United States. Surrounded by dry land, Havasu Canyon boasts a sparkling creek and towering waterfalls. This water also makes the canyon a perfect place for the Havasupai to farm in the spring and summer months. It is also a great place to swim and cool off on hot days.

Havasu Creek comes from an underground spring. The water comes up between the rocks. The temperature stays around 70 degrees Fahrenheit because the water comes from underground. The water stays cool even when summer temperatures get as high as 100 degrees Fahrenheit.

As it runs through the canyon on its way to the Colorado River, the creek makes four large waterfalls that drop into deep pools. These pools are surrounded by smaller pools, all of which contain the same beautiful blue-green water. The people who live here are named for the water. *Havasupai* means "people of the blue-green water."

The water only looks blue-green. Tiny bits of white rock called limestone are mixed in the water. When the limestone settles on the bottom of the creek, the stone reflects the blue sky. This makes the water look blue-green.

The limestone that settles out of the water also makes dams. These dams form the pools at the bottom of each waterfall and more pools all along Havasu Creek. The waterfalls' spray also tosses bits of lime into the air. Some bits stick to the rocks and form ledges. These ledges hang beneath and alongside the falls.

**Limestone dams and pools beneath Havasu Falls**

Each of the waterfalls has a name. Havasu Falls is considered the most beautiful. Mooney Falls is the highest at 190 feet. Navajo Falls is the smallest at 70 feet. A few miles from the town center is Beaver Falls.

The falls make Havasu Canyon one of the most beautiful spots in the Grand Canyon. For the people who live here, this unspoiled beauty is a source of great happiness. However, living here has its problems, too. Ever since the Havasupai made the canyon their home hundreds of years ago, they have struggled to protect it and keep it unspoiled.

## HAVASUPAI FACT

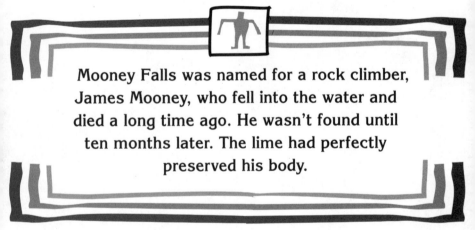

Mooney Falls was named for a rock climber, James Mooney, who fell into the water and died a long time ago. He wasn't found until ten months later. The lime had perfectly preserved his body.

# An Ancient People

Where did the Havasupai come from? Why did they decide to live at the bottom of a canyon? The story begins a long time ago.

Ancestors of the Havasupai were called the Cohonina (koh hoh NEE nuh). In the 1200s they lived on the plateaus of what is today northern Arizona. They had come here from northern Mexico, where people were fighting over land and food.

**Plateaus along the Grand Canyon**

The Cohonina brought what they knew about farming to the plateaus. Others who had lived there before the Cohonina had not been farmers. They had hunted animals and gathered nuts and berries for food instead. Some of them learned to farm from the Cohonina people.

When the Cohonina first moved to the plateaus, much more rain fell in this part of Arizona than usually falls today. They thought the soil of the plateaus would be good for farming, so they settled there. Over time, less and less rain fell. The plateaus became very dry. In time the plateaus were too dry for farming.

Several groups of Native Americans lived in the area. They began to fight over the small areas that were still good for farming. The Cohonina had moved from Mexico to these plateaus to live peacefully. They didn't want to fight, so they moved away again to look for other lands they could farm.

One of the places the Cohonina went was into the deep canyons. There they found a beautiful place with blue-green pools and waterfalls. They decided to stay there.

The Cohonina became the people we call the Havasupai today. The name comes from the way the Cohonina described themselves after they moved into the canyon. They said they were *ha vasua baaja* (hah vah SOO ah BAH hah), which meant "people of the blue-green water" in their language. People who came to this area later said their name as *Havasupai*.

**A young Havasupai girl**

The number of Havasupai grew over the years. Some thought there were too many people in the canyon. They thought the tribe should move again. The Havasupai today have a legend that tells what happened to two of the people who decided to leave.

A Havasupai couple was sad about leaving their beloved canyon. After climbing up the rocky canyon walls, they looked back. Instantly, they were turned to stone. The Havasupai believe that the two rock towers that stand above their canyon are those people.

**The Watchers standing over Havasu Canyon**

**Supai Village in Havasu Canyon**

The story says the towers became guardian spirits called the Wigleeva, or the Watchers. They watch over the people in the canyon. The Havasupai fear that their tribe will come to an end if the towers are ever destroyed.

Another legend tells how the Havasupai decided not to leave the canyon. Once, when they began to leave, a baby being carried started to cry. When the people stopped, the baby was quiet. When they started to move, the baby cried again. The people decided this was a sign that the canyon was their home.

15

By 1400, the Havasupai began to live both in the canyon and on the plateaus. They made winter homes on the plateaus that they returned to each year. Every summer they went back down into the canyon.

In the canyon the people farmed where water from the creek made the soil fertile. To bring water to their crops, they built large dams and canals. They grew corn, squash, melons, and beans. Because they were good farmers, they grew enough food to store for the winter.

**The Havasupai still farm in their canyon.**

As autumn approached, the days grew colder and shorter. By wintertime, daylight could be as short as six hours because of the shadows cast by the walls of the narrow canyon. It was time to move up onto the plateaus.

On the plateaus the Havasupai hunted deer, antelope, and small animals for food. They also visited the canyon to get food they had stored there. When the snow fell, the people had water. The trees provided firewood and branches for building homes.

## HAVASUPAI FACT

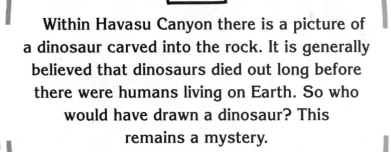

**Within Havasu Canyon there is a picture of a dinosaur carved into the rock. It is generally believed that dinosaurs died out long before there were humans living on Earth. So who would have drawn a dinosaur? This remains a mystery.**

# Chapter 3

# Friends and Enemies

While they lived peacefully in the canyon, the Havasupai met and traded with other nearby Native Americans. Some of the things the Havasupai had to trade were baskets, paint made from the red rock of their canyon walls, and soft white buckskins made from the hides of deer they hunted during the winter.

A Havasupai girl weaves a cottonwood basket while watching a young child.

**A woman weaves a Hopi blanket.**

The Hopi (HOH pee) were some of the neighbors who traded with the Havasupai. They lived on the mesas to the east of Havasu Canyon. Mesas are flat lands on top of large, tall towers of rock. The two groups were friends for hundreds of years. The Hopi traded for Havasupai baskets. In return the Havasupai received Hopi jewelry, blankets, and pottery.

The tribes respected each other. Both had ancient stories that the first people originally came out of a side canyon of the Grand Canyon. For this reason the Hopi believed Havasu Canyon to be a sacred place.

In the 1500s more people came to these plateaus and side canyons of the Grand Canyon. These new people traveled on horses, animals never before seen in these lands. These visitors came from Spain. They came because they had heard there were cities made of gold to be found here.

The people from Spain spent two years searching for gold. They left after finding none. They left behind some of their horses. In time, these animals became very important to the Havasupai and other Native Americans.

**Horses are important to the Hopi and the Havasupai.**

**Modern day Havasupai boys eat some of the peaches that grow in Havasu Canyon.**

Years later, the Spaniards returned to make the land theirs. They fought the Hopi for the land. When the Hopi were forced to leave some of their mesas, many of them found safety in the Havasupai's remote canyon.

The Hopi turned again to the Havasupai when a terrible drought made it impossible for them to farm on the mesas they still had. The Havasupai welcomed their friends. They shared their food, including the peaches that grew in their canyon.

21

The Havasupai and the Navajo (NAHV uh hoh) also were longtime friends. The Havasupai traded with the Navajo when both were on the plateaus. They also gave peaches to the Navajo when dry weather made it hard for the Navajo to farm. From this friendship grew a story that tells why one of the great Havasupai chiefs was called Navajo.

The Navajo had found a young boy wandering alone. They raised him in their tribe as a Navajo until one day a Hopi trader recognized that the boy was a Havasupai and helped the boy return to his home in the canyon. The Havasupai welcomed him back and named him "the Navajo." Years later he became a great chief. He also taught his people a Navajo song to make the horses swift, which the Havasupai sing to this day.

Even though the Havasupai had many friends among other Native Americans, some tribes were not so friendly. During the 1800s the Yavapai (YAH vuh pye) often raided the Havasupai homes and tried to take their land. The Havasupai were able to fight these enemies and drive them away.

Soon a group of unwelcome visitors arrived who also wanted the Havasupai's land. There were many of these people, and they had stronger weapons. They would force the Havasupai to stay in their canyon and would not let them use the plateaus.

A past chief of the Havasupai is Chief Watahomagie (*front*).

## HAVASUPAI FACT

Though the Hopi and the Havasupai were good friends, they were not allowed to marry each other. Hopi tradition requires married couples to stay with the wife's people. Havasupai couples stay with the husband's people.

# This Land Is Our Land

A group of unwelcome visitors appeared one autumn when the Havasupai returned to their winter home on the plateaus. The visitors were ranchers grazing their cows and sheep on the plateaus. Instead of letting the Havasupai move into their winter homes, these newcomers demanded that the Havasupai leave.

**Railroad tracks crossed much of the western territories by 1850.**

The Havasupai tried to live alongside the ranchers. Then more new people came who wanted to make money from the land by building railroads and digging mines. They told the Havasupai they could no longer live on the land that had been their home for so long.

The ranchers and miners wanted the United States government to help them push the Havasupai off the land on the plateaus. For a long time the government did not want to be a part of this struggle. Then in 1866, the United States Congress gave the Atlantic and Pacific Railroad the right to build their railroad through the Havasupai lands on the plateaus. This gave the people a bigger reason to try to drive the Havasupai away from their lands. The Havasupai finally retreated to their canyon.

Twenty years later the railroad still had not been completed. There was no money left to finish it. Even though the railroad would not run through the area, no one wanted to give the land back to the Native Americans. Cattle ranchers and settlers had already made their homes on the land. They would not leave.

The Havasupai tried peacefully to return to their land on the plateaus every year, even though they knew they would have trouble. They never fought with the people who had moved there. The Havasupai were driven off again and again, and were not even allowed to approach any of the few sources of water in the area.

Things got worse on June 8, 1880. President Rutherford B. Hayes signed an executive order that restricted the Havasupai to a small area called a reservation. A reservation is an area of land reserved, or set aside, for special use. This reservation was for Native Americans. It included only Havasu Canyon and a very small part of the plateau.

The plateau land left to the Havasupai soon became useless for hunting. The nearby herds of cattle, flocks of sheep, miners, and tourists drove away the animals that had been the Havasupai's winter source of food. The grasses that had fed the wild animals were eaten up by the animals brought by the ranchers.

Then the Havasupai began to have trouble with their Navajo friends. In the 1860s, thousands of Navajo had been captured by U.S. Army forces and pushed off their land. They were sent to live on a reservation much smaller than the home they were used to. The Havasupai, Navajo, and other tribes began to compete for the little bit of land left to them.

**Cattle brought by ranchers left little food for the wild animals that roamed the plateaus.**

A few years later, in 1893, the U.S. government realized that development could ruin the beauty of this land. To save it, they made much of the land the Grand Canyon Forest Reserve. The plateaus used by the Havasupai were part of the Reserve.

The government ordered that no Native Americans would be allowed on the land for fear they would hunt the few wild animals that were left. This angered the Havasupai. They had hunted these animals for hundreds of years without shrinking the size of the herds or ruining the land.

The Havasupai sent many letters to the U.S. government, telling them that their tribe did not have enough land. Finally, it seemed that the government listened. Part of the Grand Canyon Forest Reserve was renamed the Coconino National Forest. Though the government would not return these plateau lands to the Havasupai, they did allow them to use 100,000 acres for grazing their horses. Unfortunately, this agreement did not last.

In 1919, the government created the Grand Canyon National Park. This new park plan took away all the Havasupai's land in the reserve. The Havasupai had only their canyon left.

The Havasupai began to worry they might lose their canyon, too. The people who managed the park thought that Havasu Canyon would add to the value of the park for tourism. They said there was no room left for the Havasupai.

Tourists visit the Grand Canyon in the late 1800s.

## HAVASUPAI FACT

In 1910, the river at the bottom of the Grand Canyon flooded. The rising water wiped out all of the homes and farms in the canyon. The U.S. government rebuilt the Havasupai's homes, but they were poorly built. The Havasupai used the new buildings only to store grain.

# The Will to Survive

In the early 1900s the Havasupai almost disappeared. They had lost most of their land, and their tribe shrank to its smallest size ever, to about 250 people. Many of the people had gotten sick and died from diseases brought by settlers from outside the canyon.

**Havasupai girl of the early 1900s**

The Havasupai had to find new ways to make their living without their land for hunting or for collecting grasses for making baskets. Their skill as horseback riders helped. Some found work as packers for miners and mail carriers.

Having to spend winters in the canyon resulted in further problems. Havasu Canyon never had enough trees to supply wood for winter fires. The Havasupai solved their problem by planting fast-growing cottonwood trees. These trees could survive with little water and provided firewood and lumber for building. Today large cottonwood trees still line the pathways and surround people's homes.

**Hikers walk beneath cottonwood trees lining pathways in Havasu Canyon.**

31

Beginning in the 1960s more and more tourists began to visit the canyon. These visitors needed guides to take them down into the canyon. The tribe also built a place for visitors to stay in the canyon. This brought more money to the tribe.

During this time, Havasupai leaders increased their efforts to have their homelands returned to them. They found a powerful helper in Arizona senator Barry Goldwater.

In 1974, the Havasupai tribal council hired a lawyer and sent some of their members to the U.S. government in Washington, D.C. At first, no one in Washington would listen to the Havasupai. Then Senator Goldwater asked his friends in the government to work on the Havasupai's problem.

**Senator Barry Goldwater, 1974**

It still took a long time for something to happen. Finally, on January 4, 1975, President Gerald Ford signed a paper. It returned the Havasupai winter homelands to them, created a reservation

**President Gerald Ford, 1975**

of 188,077 acres, and gave them the right to use an additional 93,500 acres. This was the largest amount of land ever returned to a native tribe. Once again the Havasupai families could live both in the canyon and on the plateaus.

## HAVASUPAI FACT

The Havasupai still take care of the cottonwood trees planted so long ago. Each family owns its own tree, cutting some of the wood about every three years. When an elder dies, a younger family member inherits the tree.

# Chapter 6

# Growing Up Havasupai

Life in Havasu Canyon is much the same today as it has always been. For Havasupai kids, swimming, horseback riding, and, of course, school are big parts of their lives.

If you were a kid living in Havasu Canyon, the pools around the blue-green waterfalls would probably be some of your favorite spots. Here you would swim with your friends and find relief from the summer heat.

**Havasu children swimming in pools**

**Older Havasupai children care for younger ones.**

Because the Havasupai are isolated from other people, they feel safe in their quiet canyon. Children enjoy a great deal of freedom. They can leave their homes in the morning and not return until supper. At lunchtime, parents feed any children who come to their homes.

Older children are often in charge of their younger brothers and sisters. If they're under five, young children are forbidden to swim in the pools beneath the waterfalls without an older person watching them. This is a rule all the children are careful to obey. Visitors have noticed the kindness and care the young ones receive from their older brothers and sisters.

If you were a Havasupai child, you would know how to ride a horse. Your family might even own several horses. Both boys and girls ride and help care for the horses.

You probably would enjoy going to the rodeo, too. Rodeos are exciting events where people compete to see who is the most skilled at riding a horse. Events include trying to stay on a horse that tries to throw the rider off and catching a calf with a rope while riding a horse.

**Havasupai boy on a horse**

**A Havasupai rodeo contestant ties a calf's feet with rope.**

The Peach Festival held every August is a favorite event. For over a hundred years, the Havasupai have celebrated their plentiful peach harvest. During the festival, tribal dances are performed, delicious meals are cooked, and the old stories and songs are told and sung.

The Peach Festival continues to be enjoyed by many. The Havasupai still invite their neighbors, the Hopi and the Navajo. Tourists flock to the festival as well.

Like all children, Havasupai children go to school. They go to school in the canyon when they're young. Older children have to leave the canyon and go away to school. They go to boarding schools in California and Arizona, where they live and take classes during the school year.

A classroom in the Supai school looks like many other classrooms.

There is only one school in Supai for kindergarten through eighth grade. The Havasupai are very happy to have this school. For many years they had a much smaller school for just the youngest grades. For a few years, Supai had no school at all.

In the 1950s the government closed some Native American schools when there were very few students or when there was not enough money to keep them open. When the school in Supai closed, children as young as age six were sent away to live at a boarding school.

The Havasupai tried to get neighboring communities to take their children in their schools, but they refused. For nine years after their school was closed, Havasupai children were sent to school in a place called Fort Apache (uh PACH ee). This was 350 miles from their home.

Finally, in 1964, the Havasupai were able to reopen their school. The school had only two grades. Still, it meant that the children in grades one and two could stay home instead of going to Fort Apache.

The Havasupai tribe has controlled their own school system since 1966. They received a grant to build the modern school Havasupai children now attend. The people still are not completely happy with the school situation. After eighth grade, students leave the canyon to go to school. Some worry that their young people will forget their tribe's traditions while they are away.

**Havasupai schoolchildren today**

Besides school subjects such as reading and math, the children who attend school in the canyon also study the legends, culture, and traditions of their tribe. They learn about the plants and animals in Havasu Canyon. Children work on projects to help protect the canyon. They also collect fossils and study the canyon's ancient history. Havasupai children learn from the adults that preserving their sacred land is very important.

## HAVASUPAI FACT

Long ago the Peach Festival was held in September before the Havasupai moved to the plateau for the winter. When the Havasupai were confined to their canyon and older children went to boarding school, the festival was moved to August. The festival reminds children of their traditions before they leave for school.

# Havasu Canyon Today

Today the Havasupai still must struggle to keep their traditions alive. They were able to keep their language, celebrations, and religious beliefs strong in part because they lived in a remote canyon that few people visited. Now, thousands of tourists visit each year and bring with them the outside world and an outside culture.

**A tourist enjoys the sparkling pools**

**Tourists ride Havasupai mules on the canyon trails.**

Many visitors hike or ride down the eight-mile trail to Havasu Canyon. Some of the Havasupai work as pack leaders. They rent their horses or mules to people who want to make the difficult journey down to Supai by riding. Then they lead these tourists down the path.

It is also possible now for people to hire a helicopter to take them down to the canyon floor. Some people don't like the helicopters because they make so much noise and stir up so much dust in the canyon.

In Supai Village, visitors can stay at a 24-room lodge run by the Havasupai. There is also a cafe and a museum that sells tribal crafts.

The Havasupai welcome tourists, but they may not greet each one. They value their privacy. They ask that visitors stay off their sacred lands and use only the trails and campgrounds open to them. The Havasupai also ask that tourists do not disturb their children by taking their photographs.

**The lodge at Supai Village**

People who visit Havasu Canyon hear and see that the Havasupai live both in their traditional world and in the modern world. Along the paths they hear both the Havasupai language and English spoken, sometimes in the same sentence. Most of the the older people still use the native language.

Supai still receives its mail the old way. It's the only post office left in the country that receives its mail by mule. Until a few years ago, this was the only way to stay in touch with people in the canyon. Then, in 1995, the first computer was flown into the village by helicopter. The tribe was connected to the Internet and could send and receive messages electronically, or by e-mail. Because there are still only a few phone lines, Internet access is slow.

Even with their lands returned, the Havasupai still face many problems. Terrible rains caused damaging floods in 1993, 1995, and the worst one of all in August of 1997. The canyon had not experienced a flood as big as the one in 1997 for 80 years. A bulldozer had to be flown into the canyon to help clean up.

Havasupai tribal leaders as well as scientists worry that this new weather pattern may be a result of worldwide global warming. Some people believe that this rise in the earth's temperature is brought on by pollution from factories and big cities. Now members of the Havasupai tribal council have to watch what is happening beyond their canyon so they can plan ways to protect their homes once again.

Mining on their land is a problem for the Havasupai as well. Uranium, a chemical used in nuclear reactors, has been found in the rock around Havasu Canyon. Mining companies want to set up equipment to take the uranium out of the ground so they can sell it. Since the 1980s the Havasupai have been trying to convince the U.S. government to stop this from happening. The Havasupai believe mines will pollute their water supply and hurt the natural environment. They are worried about how this will affect their people as well as the plants and animals on Havasupai land.

Havasu Canyon is a place you may like to visit one day. When you go, keep in mind the history of the people who have cared for the land for so many years. Their legends and traditions are part of the rocky cliffs.

If you hike the trails and swim in the beautiful blue-green pools, remember that the land around you is someone else's home. It's a home a people have fought to protect for a very long time.

A Havasupai man greets a visitor in the lodge.

## HAVASUPAI FACT

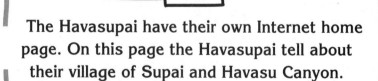

The Havasupai have their own Internet home page. On this page the Havasupai tell about their village of Supai and Havasu Canyon.

# Glossary

**Fahrenheit** [FAR un hyt] a measure of temperature on a thermometer in which the freezing point is 32 degrees above zero and the boiling point is 212 degrees

**grant** [grant] something that is given, such as money, for a particular purpose

**grazing** [GRAYZ ihng] feeding on growing grass or other plants in pastures

**harvest** [HAR vust] a crop of grain or fruit that has been gathered after ripening

**legend** [LEJ und] a story handed down through the years that is connected with some real events

**mesas** [MAY suz] large, high rocks, having steep sides and a flat top

**plateaus** [pla TOHZ] broad stretches of high, level land

**reflects** [rih FLEKTS] gives back an image of, as in a mirror

**remote** [rih MOHT] far off or far away from a particular place; distant

**sacred** [SAY krud] having to do with religion; given or deserving the greatest respect